THE LAUGHTER CURE

A MINI-GUIDE TO LIGHTEN ANY LOAD

BY RODOLFO RABONZA

Author: Rodolfo Rabonza
Illustrations: Pine Tree Press
Formatting: Pine Tree Press
Copyright: ©2025 By Rodolfo Rabonza
All Rights Reserved.

No part of this book may be reproduced, distributed, or transmitted in any form or by any means, including photocopying, recording, or other electronic or mechanical methods, without the prior written permission of the publisher, except in the case of brief quotations embodied in critical reviews and certain other noncommercial uses permitted by copyright law. For permission requests, write to the publisher at the address below.

Published by Pine Tree Press

www.pinetreepress.com
Printed in USA

A MINI-GUIDE TO LIGHTEN ANY LOAD

Table of Contents

01 Why Seriousness Makes Everything Heavier

02 The Science of Laughter

03 The Art of Making It Ridiculous

04 The 60-Second Grin Reset

05 Laughing at Your Calendar

06 Decision Fatigue Antidote

07 Humor as Leadership

08 Defusing Tension

09 Building Trust Through Play

10 The Legacy of Laughter

11 Humor as Daily Wealth

12 Your Personal Laughter Ritual

DEDICATION

To everyone who forgot how to laugh—

and to those who reminded me it was the only way forward.

For the dreamers carrying too much,

the achievers forgetting to breathe,

and the souls learning that lightness is wisdom.

ACKNOWLEDGMENT

- This book exists because of laughter shared in hard moments.
- To my family, thank you for believing, supporting, and forgiving my endless curiosity.
- To my friends and travel companions who filled my journeys with joy and perspective, you made the world lighter.
- To my mentors, spiritual guides, and every person who sparked a conversation that led to a new insight, thank you for shaping the way I see life.
- And to you, the Reader: May this book remind you that your lightness is your strength.

A MINI-GUIDE TO LIGHTEN ANY LOAD

Introduction

On the Space Between Ourselves and Our Sorrows

Before anything else, let me say this plainly:
I am not a master of laughter, nor do I pretend to be.
I am simply a student of the mind — my own, first of all — and of the strange ways it traps itself.

What you will find in these pages is not a promise of constant cheerfulness, nor a demand to smile through hardship. It is something quieter, older, and far more human: the recognition that our attention shapes the world we experience.

When our attention becomes fixed on a single worry, grievance, or fear, the world seems to shrink around that one thing. We lose our sense of proportion. We lose our space. And in that contraction, we begin to act from pressure rather than clarity, from fear rather than freedom.

Philosophers have long taught that wisdom begins with perspective — the ability to step back, to widen the frame, to see the larger movement of life in which our troubles are only small notes in a vast composition.

Laughter, as humble as it seems, is one of the simplest ways to reclaim that perspective.
Not the loud, performative laughter of shows and crowds, but the subtle softening of the mind — the small release that reminds us we are more than the moment that holds us.

This book is an invitation to explore that space:
the space between ourselves and our sorrows,
between our awareness and our disturbances,
between who we are and what we momentarily face.

I won't reveal everything here.
Discovery is part of the journey.

All I will say is this:

If you can gently shift your attention, even for a breath, you may begin to see life not as a narrow corridor of problems, but as a vast landscape through which you move with greater presence, clarity, and grace.

If that interests you, turn the page.
A wider view awaits.

- Rodolfo Rabonza

PART I

THE PERSPECTIVE SHIFT

A MINI-GUIDE TO LIGHTEN ANY LOAD

Chapter 1
Why Seriousness Makes Everything Heavier

A MINI-GUIDE TO LIGHTEN ANY LOAD

"*Man suffers not only from the things themselves, but from the way he views them.*"
-Epictetus

"*If you are irritated by every rub, how will your mirror be polished?*"
-Rumi

INSIGHT

The truth is, most of what weighs us down isn't the situation itself, but the seriousness we wrap around it. Money magnifies this. A missed opportunity, a deal gone sideways, a family request you can't dodge – it all feels monumental. But seriousness is like pouring concrete on top of a balloon. It stops the natural lift. A child laughs 300 times a day. An adult? Maybe 20. Not because life got harder, but because we decided to be 'serious.'

EXAMPLE

After losing $16 billion in a single day, Elon Musk shrugged it off with a Monty Python quote: "Always look on the bright side of life." That's classic Musk unshaken and irreverent. Even in 2023, after seeing more than $100 billion vanish, he was still joking not about the loss, but about life itself. It's a reminder that true freedom isn't measured by fortune, but by perspective, attitude, and the ability to laugh when life turns absurd. And now, in 2025, he's on track to become the world's first trillionaire.

A MINI-GUIDE TO LIGHTEN ANY LOAD

MANTRA

**Lightness is power.
Heaviness is a trap.**

EXERCISE

Pick one thing you're taking seriously today. Write down the worst-case scenario. Now exaggerate it until it's absurd. (If a meeting goes wrong, imagine everyone wearing clown shoes. If you lose money, imagine explaining it to aliens.) Notice the weight dissolves.

WHAT DID YOU NOTICE?

_____

_____

_____

_____

_____

Chapter 2

The Science of Laughter

"No man is free who is not master of himself."
-Epictetus

"The mind is not a vessel to be filled but a fire to be kindled."
-Plutarch

INSIGHT

Laughter releases endorphins. It lowers cortisol. It increases resilience. In boardrooms or living rooms, humor reboots the nervous system. You think clearer. You connect faster.

EXAMPLE

Google found that teams with the most laughter in meetings also had the highest productivity. The data backs what comedians and monks already knew: A light heart thinks better.

MANTRA

Every laugh is a reset button.

EXERCISE

Today, watch or listen to something funny for two minutes before your next important decision. Notice how much easier your mind flows afterward.

WHAT DID YOU NOTICE?

_____

_____

_____

_____

_____

Chapter 3

The Art of Making It Ridiculous

A MINI-GUIDE TO LIGHTEN ANY LOAD

"It is the power of the mind to be unconquerable."
-Seneca

"Life is like a play: It matters not how long it is, but how well it is acted."
-Seneca

INSIGHT

The great spiritual trick: If you can laugh at it, you're not trapped by it.

EXAMPLE

A billionaire, worried about legacy, once joked: "My kids will either honor me...or sell everything and buy an island. Either way, I'll be remembered." Humor transforms fear into play.

MANTRA

When you laugh at it,
you loosen its grip.

EXERCISE

Take one current tension. Rewrite it as a ridiculous headline: 'CEO Panics Over Paperclip Shortage.' 'Investor Conquered by Coffee Stain.' Read it out loud. Laugh at how small it really is.

WHAT DID YOU NOTICE?

_____
_____
_____
_____
_____

A MINI-GUIDE TO LIGHTEN ANY LOAD

PART II

EVERYDAY PRACTICES

Chapter 4

The 60-Second Grin Reset

A MINI-GUIDE TO LIGHTEN ANY LOAD

"Very little is needed to make a happy life; it is all within yourself."
-Marcus Aurelius

"Happiness depends upon ourselves."
-Aristotle

INSIGHT

Your body fools your brain. Smile for 60 seconds, even fake, and your brain releases happy chemicals.

EXAMPLE

Winston Churchill, during war councils, would sometimes crack a half-smile mid-crisis. A staffer said, "That tiny grin made us believe we could win."

MANTRA

My smile is my reset.

EXERCISE

Set a timer. Smile (even forced) for one minute. Repeat anytime tension builds.

WHAT DID YOU NOTICE?

_____

_____

_____

_____

_____

Chapter 5

Laughing at Your Calendar

"The whole life of man is but a point of time; let us enjoy it."
—Plutarch

"We must make the best of those things that are in our power, and take the rest as nature gives it."
—Epictetus

INSIGHT

We all feel 'scheduled to death.' Meetings, flights, dinners, calls. The wealthy have endless demands; so do students. Same energy. The trick? See your calendar as a comedy lineup. Each appointment is just an 'act' on stage.

EXAMPLE

Imagine a billionaire investor introducing his 7:30 a.m. breakfast meeting: "Up next, the thrilling PowerPoint on quarterly growth, give them a round of applause!"

MANTRA

My day is a comedy show, not a cage.

EXERCISE

Look at tomorrow's calendar. Write a silly nickname for each item. Notice how the stress shifts into play.

WHAT DID YOU NOTICE?

_____

_____

_____

_____

_____

Chapter 6
Decision Fatigue Antidote

"He is a wise man who does not grieve for the things he has not, but rejoices for those which he has."
— Epictetus

"The soul becomes dyed with the color of its thoughts."
— Marcus Aurelius

INSIGHT

Too many decisions kill energy.
Humor revives it.

EXAMPLE

Jeff Bezos once said he tries to make only three high-quality decisions a day. Imagine the rest as absurd: "Should I wear the blue socks or the spaceship socks?"

MANTRA

Laugh, then decide.

EXERCISE

Before your next big decision, ask: "What would a five-year-old say about this?" Use the laughter to cut through the fog.

WHAT DID YOU NOTICE?

_____

_____

_____

_____

_____

PART III

RELATIONSHIPS & INFLUENCE

Chapter 7
Humor as Leadership

A MINI-GUIDE TO LIGHTEN ANY LOAD

"The first and greatest victory is to conquer yourself."
—Plutarch

"The key is to keep company only with people who uplift you, whose presence calls forth your best."
—Epictetus

"It is the peculiar quality of a fool to perceive the faults of others and to forget his own."
—Cicero

INSIGHT

Leaders who can laugh with their teams build loyalty. Humor says: "We're human first, titles second."

EXAMPLE

Richard Branson dressed as a flight attendant for a bet. His empire didn't shrink, his people adored him more.

MANTRA

Humor lifts people up and it leads.

EXERCISE

Share one light joke in your next meeting. Notice how quickly walls come down.

WHAT DID YOU NOTICE?

_____

_____

_____

_____

_____

Chapter 8

Defusing Tension

A MINI-GUIDE TO LIGHTEN ANY LOAD

"Anger, if not restrained, is frequently more hurtful to us than the injury that provokes it."
—Seneca

"Better to trip with the feet than with the tongue."
—Zeno of Citium

"He who laughs, lasts."
—Ancient Roman Proverb

INSIGHT

Arguments escalate because of seriousness. Humor interrupts the pattern.

EXAMPLE

A couple in a fight paused when the husband put on a fake cowboy hat mid-argument. They laughed, and the fight dissolved.

MANTRA

Tension dies in laughter.

EXERCISE

Next conflict, insert something playful (a funny phrase, a silly gesture). Watch the mood shift.

WHAT DID YOU NOTICE?

_____

_____

_____

_____

_____

Chapter 9
Building Trust Through Play

"Friendship is a single soul dwelling in two bodies."
—Aristotle

"The good life is one inspired by love and guided by knowledge."
—Bertrand Russell

INSIGHT

Laughter is a shortcut to trust. It lowers defenses instantly.

EXAMPLE

A Fortune 500 CEO said his best deals happened not in the boardroom but over shared laughter at dinner.

MANTRA

Shared laughter is shared trust.

EXERCISE

Today, find one opportunity to make someone laugh not by force, but by lightness. Observe how his guard lowers.

WHAT DID YOU NOTICE?

_____

_____

_____

_____

_____

A MINI-GUIDE TO LIGHTEN ANY LOAD

PART IV

LIVING LIGHT

A MINI-GUIDE TO LIGHTEN ANY LOAD

Chapter 10

The Legacy of Laughter

"Waste no more time arguing about what a good man should be.
Be one."
—Marcus Aurelius

"What we leave behind is not what is engraved in stone monuments,
but what is woven into the lives of others."
—Pericles

INSIGHT

At the end of life, what people remember isn't your net worth, it's the moments you made them smile.

EXAMPLE

Steve Jobs was remembered not just for the iPhone, but for the moments he made colleagues laugh in presentations.

MANTRA

Legacy is measured in laughter.

EXERCISE

Write down one memory where laughter changed your relationship. That's part of your legacy already.

WHAT DID YOU NOTICE?

_____
_____
_____
_____
_____

Chapter 11
Humor as Daily Wealth

"Wealth consists not in having great possessions, but in having few wants."
— Epictetus

"If you are not satisfied with a little, you will never be satisfied with much."
— Epicurus

"The happy man is he who has wise thoughts."
— Democritus

INSIGHT

True wealth isn't money, it's energy, connection, joy. Humor multiplies all three.

EXAMPLE

When the author Norman Cousins became seriously ill, the outlook wasn't promising. Instead of sinking into fear, he decided to experiment with something unconventional: laughter. He checked himself into a hotel room, gathered a stack of old comedy films, and spent hours watching anything that could make him genuinely laugh. What he noticed was remarkable—after a solid stretch of real, belly-deep laughter, he could sleep for hours without pain. It became his daily ritual.
Cousins later said that those moments of joy were one of the most healing forces he had.

MANTRA

Laughter is my daily dividend.

A MINI-GUIDE TO LIGHTEN ANY LOAD

EXERCISE

Count your laughs today. Aim for 50. Yes, even if you need to watch cat videos.

WHAT DID YOU NOTICE?

_____

_____

_____

_____

_____

Chapter 12
Your Personal Laughter Ritual

A MINI-GUIDE TO LIGHTEN ANY LOAD

"The art of living is more like wrestling than dancing."
— Marcus Aurelius

"Begin at once to live, and count each day as a separate life."
— Seneca

"The unexamined life is not worth living."
— Socrates

INSIGHT

End every day by finding the funniest thing that happened. That's your ritual.

EXAMPLE

Oprah said she keeps a gratitude journal. A 'laughter journal' works the same way.

MANTRA

I end the day lighter than I began.

EXERCISE

Tonight, write down your funniest moment of the day. Do it daily for 21 days. Notice your mood lift.

WHAT DID YOU NOTICE?

_____
_____
_____
_____
_____

Epilogue

The View From Higher Ground

I want to leave you with something simple and honest:
I don't claim to be a laughter guru.
I don't walk around cackling all day.
And if you met me on an ordinary afternoon, you might even wonder how I ever wrote a book on laughter in the first place.

But that's exactly the point.

Laughter, to me, is not a personality. It's not a performance.
It's a tool — a practical, immediate way to unfix your attention from whatever has you trapped.

Because when your attention gets stuck on something, your power shrinks.
Your space shrinks.
You get pulled right up against the problem until it fills your entire field of vision.
And from that cramped viewpoint, every decision feels heavier, urgent, distorted - never the optimal one.

Laughter breaks that spell.
It gives you back the space you lost.
And with more space, comes clarity.
And with clarity, comes choice.

I learned this in one of the most unexpected classrooms of my life: the trail to Everest Base Camp.

The higher I climbed, the more the world changed.
Trees thinned into shrubs, and shrubs vanished into rocks.
Soon it felt like another planet – silent, raw, enormous.
And somewhere in that vast lunar landscape, I felt an overwhelming sense of aloneness, like I had stepped outside the world entirely.

Up there, far above the busy cities and schedules and expectations, something clicked.
All the games we play: money, deadlines, pressure, family demands suddenly looked tiny.
Small.
Like scattered pebbles against an ocean of mountains.

From that distance, the problems that normally feel huge turned into manageable specks.
Their magnitude shrank.
Their grip loosened.

And the same thing happens when you use laughter as a tool. It expands your space enough for you to see life from a global perspective, the long view, the whole map, the real scale of what matters.

With more space, you stop reacting and start creating.
You stop being trapped inside a cycle of "start, modify, stop" and rediscover the freedom to make new choices.
Some problems don't even need to be solved, they dissolve when you rise to a larger viewpoint.

This book was never meant to tell you to laugh your way through life. It was meant to hand you a lever, something simple, light, and human, to pry your attention loose when it gets stuck.

Laughter doesn't erase reality. It just widens it.

So take what helps you.
Use what frees you.
And remember: Sometimes the smallest chuckle can open the biggest space.

Here's to seeing life from higher ground and to making better, brighter decisions from that view.

— Rodolfo Rabonza

About the Author

Rodolfo Rabonza is a runner, traveler, and creator who believes joy is the ultimate strength. He has trekked the mountains of Patagonia, stood at the foot of Everest on the Himalayan trek to Base Camp, walked Japan's sacred Kumano Kodo, and completed two Camino de Santiago pilgrimages, one along the Portuguese route from Porto and one on the classic French Way, with a pledge to walk a new route every year. He has also run ultramarathons across continents and sat at café tables from Budapest to Tokyo. His work combines adventure, spirituality, and self-awareness, reminding us that the richest life is measured in laughter as much as in milestones.

www.ingramcontent.com/pod-product-compliance
Lightning Source LLC
Chambersburg PA
CBHW042132080426
42735CB00005B/149